IS PLASTIC MONEY REAL?

How Credit Cards Work

Math Book Nonfiction 9th Grade
Children's Money & Saving Reference

In this book, we're going to talk about how credit cards work. So, let's get right to it!

Credit cards have become a very convenient way to purchase things and they are safer than carrying cash in your wallet. They also allow you to have more time to pay for things. If they are used wisely, they can be a financial help.

However, if you're not careful with the way you use them, you can quickly get in over your head in debt.

It's not unusual for the average household in the United States to have $8000 to $16,000 or more in credit card debt that can't easily be paid off.

WHAT ARE CREDIT CARDS?

Credit cards are used so often today that it's hard to believe they weren't in existence before the 1950s. Suppose you want to buy something but you don't have the cash for it. A credit card allows you to pay for something today without spending cash to get it.

Credit Card
1234 5678 9012 3456
NAME   01/34

It's not free money. It's simply a way for you to extend the time you have to pay something back to the bank that loaned you the money on the card.

Credit cards are small plastic cards that have an account number on them. When you pay for something, the magnetic strip on the back is scanned so that the merchant can get the information to give you a receipt for your purchase.

Newer credit cards have a magnetic chip in them that can be read by a scanner. These magnetic chips have better security features and are intended to limit credit card fraud.

You are using the credit card to pay using the credit limit that a particular bank has issued to you. In other words, you are using the bank's money.

It's real money that the bank has. You are promising to pay this money back to the bank every time you use the card. Almost all merchants accept different types of credit cards, so you can use a credit card to buy just about anything, including dinner out, clothing, or a video game. If you use credit cards wisely, it helps you to establish a credit profile. If you have good credit, then it's easier to make larger purchases in the future that may require a loan, such as when you buy a car or a house.

HOW OLD DO YOU HAVE TO BE TO GET YOUR OWN CREDIT CARD?

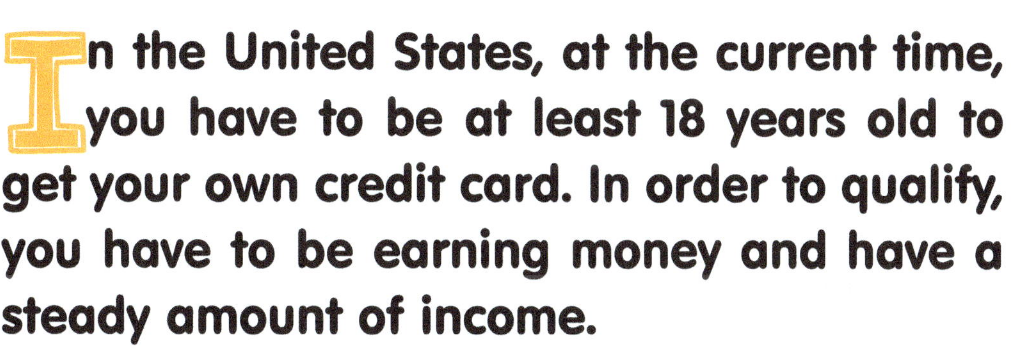

In the United States, at the current time, you have to be at least 18 years old to get your own credit card. In order to qualify, you have to be earning money and have a steady amount of income.

When you apply for a credit card, the bank wants to know that you are capable of paying the money back otherwise you won't be a good credit risk for them. A regular allowance that you get from your parents isn't seen as income by the bank. You would need to show that you have a job and are earning a regular paycheck.

A WORKING WOMAN

YOUNG WOMAN PAYING USING A
CREDIT CARD

When you apply for your very first credit card, there are just a few potential options until you establish a credit history. You can look for a credit card that is designed specifically for students or a department store credit card. It is usually a little easier to apply for these types of cards.

nother way is to get a secured credit card. This type of card is a little different since you have to put in a deposit before you can get the card.

The deposit is a portion of your credit limit so if you default on the card, the bank can take your money. It's a way for the bank to minimize its risk since you don't have a credit history yet.

If you're under 18 years old, an adult like your mom or dad can make you an authorized user on one of their credit cards. You'll have your own credit card that you can use, but they will be responsible for making the payments. Another way to use a credit card is to get a prepaid card. It looks like a credit card, but it isn't really a true credit card. That's because you have to pay it in advance.

A GIRL STUDENT HOLDING HER CREDIT CARD

In other words, you would pay $50 on a prepaid card ahead of time, then, you can use it like a credit card to pay for a $6 coffee drink. This type of card doesn't help you to establish a credit history, but it's still convenient.

USING A CREDIT CARD

There are at least four different ways that you can use credit cards to pay for something or get cash.

PAY IN PERSON

When you're in a store and you want to buy something, you present your credit card to the cashier to pay for the purchase.

The magnetic strip on the backside of the card is run through a terminal that verifies the purchase.

Sometimes if the terminal isn't working or if you aren't allowed to charge any more on that card, your purchase won't be approved.

POS TERMINAL
PAYMENT
PAY
APPROVED

PAY OVER THE PHONE OR THE INTERNET

If you buy something by using your phone or buying it on the internet, you'll have to provide specific information so that the merchant can verify you and your credit card. You'll be asked to give the number of your account as well as the month and the year that the card expires. You'll need to give your full name and address as well. There's a three-digit security number on the back of the card that you may be asked to supply.

GET CASH AT AN ATM

You can sometimes use your credit card to get cash from an Automated Teller Machine or ATM. Of course, there is a limit to the amount of cash you can get based on your credit limit and credit history. There are sometimes very high fees for this service.

USE A SPECIAL CHECK ISSUED BY THE CREDIT CARD COMPANY

Sometimes credit cards will issue checks in the mail. You can use these checks to deposit an amount from your credit limit into your bank account. Once again, the fees for this service are sometimes very high.

BANK

WHERE DOES THE MONEY COME FROM?

Suppose you have applied for a credit card and XYZ bank has approved you. XYZ bank will give you a line of credit based on your credit history. Let's say your line of credit is $3500. This means that you can charge any amount of money up to $3500, before they will deny you credit or charge you fees because you are over your limit.

You immediately go out and buy a new television set for $675. When you present the card for payment at the store, the bank will pay for your new television, but the money isn't free. Sometimes it seems that way since you didn't have to give the cashier any paper money.

When you receive the bill in the mail the next month, you'll need to pay the entire

$675 with a check from your bank account or you'll pay interest and possibly fees on the amount.

The amount of interest charged might be anywhere from 9% to as much as almost 30% or more.

If you only pay the minimum payment on your account, it will take you years to pay off that television set and it will cost hundreds or perhaps thousands more than the original amount that was charged depending on how long you take to pay it off.

STRESSED MAN IN DEBT FROM CREDIT CARD USE

MAN IN DEBT FROM CREDIT CARD USE

CREDIT CARDS MEAN DEBT

Unless you pay off your credit card bills every month, you will be in debt. You owe the money to the banks that issued you your credit cards. When you receive the bill, it will show the interest rate you are paying. It will also give you the option of sending in a minimum payment. The statement will give you the total amount that you owe.

The bank that issued you the card makes its money on the interest rate and fees that it charges you. Many people just pay the minimum amounts on their credit card bills and they have "revolving debt." They continue to pay interest on the purchases they already made and then they buy more things and owe interest on the new things they purchased as well.

A credit card doesn't have a specific end date for when it must be completely paid off so the interest is just charged every month until you pay off the bill in full.

Credit card companies use an interest rate that's called an APR or Annual Percentage Rate. They charge the rate daily and it's based on a compound interest formula. To find out how much interest you're being charged every day, take the APR for your credit card and divide it by 365 days in a year.

INTEREST RATES
BUSINESS
COMMUNICATION
ANALYSIS
FINANCE
CREATIVITY
ACCOUNTING
IMPROVEMENT
PARTNERSHIP

Interest Rates

For example, if your credit card charges you 20% interest annually, then each day the interest will be 0.05479% approximately, which is the number you get when you divide 20% by 365. Now, let's say you owe $1,000 on revolving debt.

The first day of the month that will be $1{,}000 \times 0.0005479 = 1{,}000.55$. That may not seem like a lot more but the next day it's $1{,}000.55 \times 0.0005479$ again and so on and so forth.

CREDIT CARD
1 2 3 4 5 6 7 8 9 9
JANE SMITH
VALID
THRU
09 / 15
EXCLUSIVE

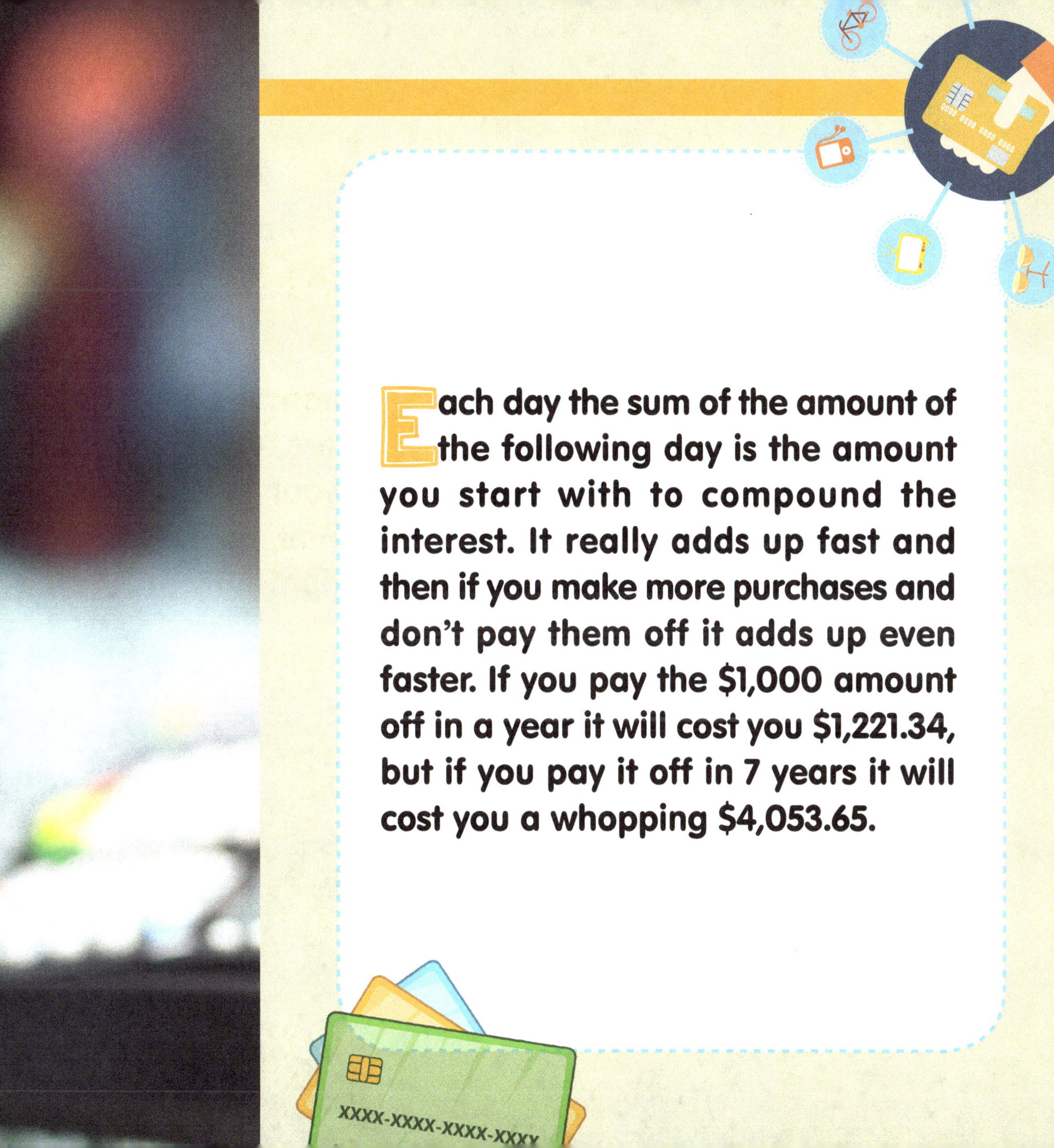

Each day the sum of the amount of the following day is the amount you start with to compound the interest. It really adds up fast and then if you make more purchases and don't pay them off it adds up even faster. If you pay the $1,000 amount off in a year it will cost you $1,221.34, but if you pay it off in 7 years it will cost you a whopping $4,053.65.

CREDIT CARD FEES

Credit cards have many different types of fees. There may be fees charged for being late with your payment, going over your credit limit, and an annual fee simply for the right to use the card.

SHOPPING BANK
GOLD MEMBER
4402
014
USA
7019
6
USA
009
6

USE CREDIT CARD RESPONSIBLY

Paying by credit card isn't free money. Although the bank that issued the credit card initially pays for your purchase, you will need to make payments and pay interest and fees until the purchase has been completely paid off.

REWARDS
3200
5404

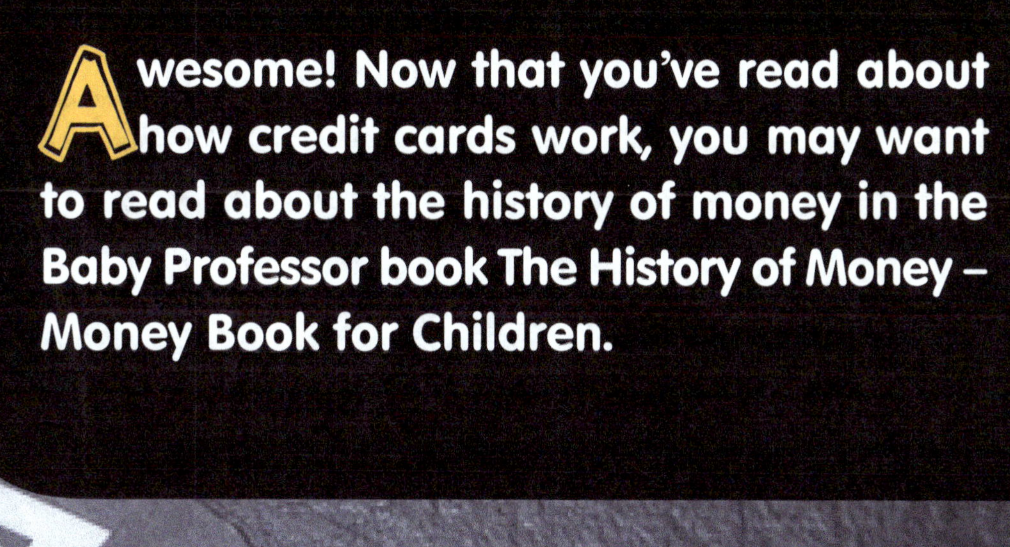

Awesome! Now that you've read about how credit cards work, you may want to read about the history of money in the Baby Professor book The History of Money – Money Book for Children.

Visit

www.BabyProfessorBooks.com
to download Free Baby Professor eBooks
and view our catalog of new and exciting
Children's Books